Great Smoky Mountains National Park

PRESERVING AMERICA

Nate Frisch

Published by
CREATIVE EDUCATION

P.O. Box 227, Mankato, Minnesota 56002
Creative Education is an imprint of The Creative Company
www.thecreativecompany.us

Design and production by Danny Nanos of Gilbert & Nanos
Art direction by Rita Marshall
Printed in the United States of America

Photographs by Alamy (Michael Hare), Getty Images (Tsoi Hoi Fung), nps.gov, Shutterstock (Solodov Alexey, Denis Barbulat, Natalia Bratslavsky, Mark Bridger, Tony Campbell, ChipPix, Ken Durden, Gencay M. Emin, Melinda Fawver, Jeffrey M. Frank, gary718, jadimages, Jose Gil, Kane513, Kapu, Iza Korwel, Krajomfire, Geir Olav Lyngfjell, Tim Mainiero, MING-HSIANG, Caitlin Mirra, mlorenz, Odua Images, pashabo, Dean Pennala, picturepartners, Jean-Edouard Rozey, Henryk Sadura, Betty Shelton, Kenneth Sponsler, StillScott, Amelia Takacs, Mary Terriberry, Timurpix, Mike Truchon, Alex Valent, Vasaleks, VR Photos, Jerry Whaley, Mark Winfrey, Ryhor M Zasinets)

Library of Congress Cataloging-in-Publication Data

Frisch, Nate.
Great Smoky Mountains National Park / by Nate Frisch.
p. cm. — (Preserving America)
Includes bibliographical references and index.
Summary: An exploration of Great Smoky Mountains National Park, including how its mountainous landscape was formed, its history of preservation, and tourist attractions such as the historic settlement called Cades Cove.

ISBN 978-1-60818-197-1
1. Great Smoky Mountains National Park (N.C. and Tenn.)—Juvenile literature. I. Title.
F443.G7F69 2013
976.8'89—dc23   2012023231

2 4 6 8 9 7 5 3

Cover & page 3: *A view across the Great Smoky Mountains; a gray squirrel*

CREATIVE EDUCATION

Great Smoky Mountains National Park

PRESERVING AMERICA

Nate Frisch

Table of Contents

TOWERING MOUNTAINS and glassy lakes. Churning rivers and dense forests. Lush prairies and baking deserts. The open spaces and natural wonders of the United States once seemed as limitless as they were diverse. But as human expansion and development increased in the 1800s, forests and prairies were replaced by settlements and agricultural lands. Waterways were diverted, wildlife was over-hunted, and the earth was scarred by mining. Fortunately, many Americans fought to preserve some of the country's vanishing wilderness. In 1872, Yellowstone National Park was established, becoming the first true national park in the world and paving the way for future preservation efforts. In 1901, Theodore Roosevelt became U.S. president. He once stated, "There can be no greater issue than that of conservation in this country," and during his presidency, Roosevelt signed five national parks into existence. The National Park Service (NPS) was created in 1916 to manage the growing number of U.S. parks. In 1934, Great Smoky Mountains National Park was established in Tennessee and North Carolina. Featuring ancient landforms and a rich diversity of plant and animal life, this misty and mountainous preserve quickly earned a place among America's most treasured parks.

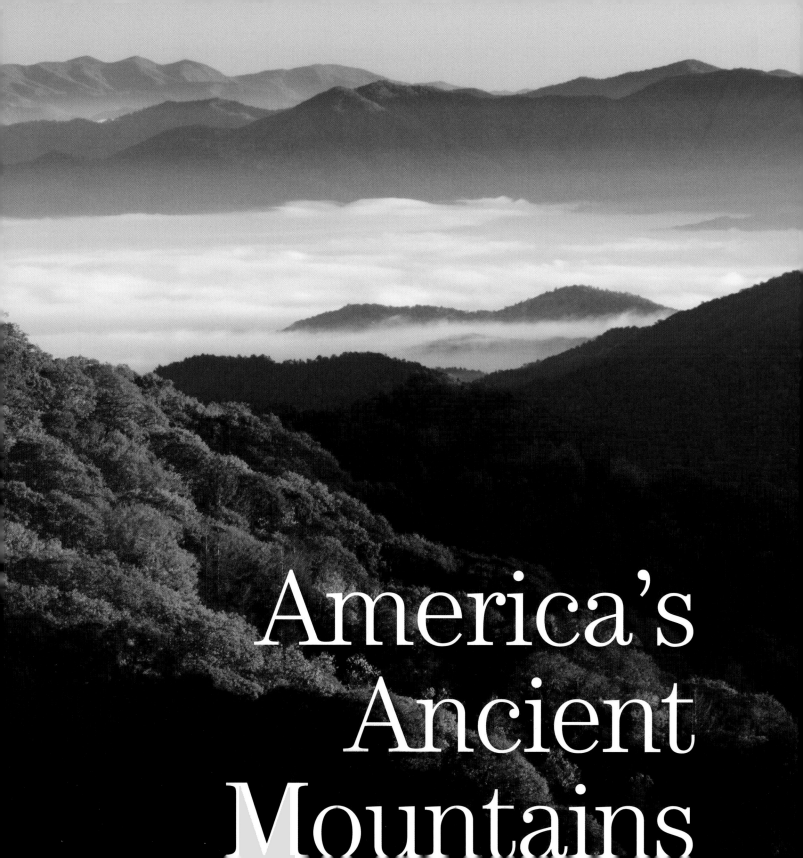

America's
Ancient
Mountains

Great Smoky Mountains National Park is split between two states: Tennessee makes up the top half, and North Carolina the bottom

As its name implies, Great Smoky Mountains National Park is indeed mountainous, as it is located along the spine of the Appalachian range. This range is very different from the sharp, craggy mountains of the Rockies, Cascades, or Sierras in the western U.S. The main difference is that the Appalachian Mountains are many times older than those western ranges.

Scientists believe the rock foundation of the Appalachians is about a billion years old. Unlike western mountain ranges that were formed relatively quickly by way of volcanic activity or shifting **faults**, the Appalachians took shape as a result of **continental drift** when **tectonic plates** collided. Some 300 million years ago, the landmasses that are now North America and Africa were very close together and drifting ever closer. While this drifting—and inevitable collision—was extremely slow, the enormous mass of the plates created so much force that the edge of the North American plate crumpled up. The effect was similar to the way the hood of a car might buckle upward during a collision, only on an incredibly huge scale. By the time the force of the colliding plates was finally redirected, the Appalachian range had risen thousands of feet above sea level and extended nearly the entire length of what is now America's eastern coast.

The process of continental drift was also responsible for the tallest mountain range on Earth, the Himalayas of south-central Asia. And although no one knows for sure, the Appalachians were quite possibly once taller than any mountain range that exists in the U.S. today. However, in the millions of years that have passed since the formation of the Appalachians, wind, rain, prying tree roots, and alternating freezing and thawing temperatures have gradually **eroded** the mountains to a fraction of their former size and worn the sharp points and edges off their peaks.

The Great Smoky Mountains represent a small portion of the 1,500-mile-long (2,414 km) Appalachians but exhibit many of the same characteristics as the rest of this ancient range. Today, the highest point in the "Smokies" is Clingmans Dome, which rises 6,643 feet (2,025 m) above sea level. Even this peak is low enough to be covered by Fraser firs, red spruce, and other **conifers**. In fact, evergreen forests almost completely blanket the higher elevations of the region. Perhaps no sight epitomizes the Great Smoky Mountains better than that of blunt, tree-covered peaks extending as far as the eye can see. As the layers extend toward the horizon, they fade in color from deep green to muted blue to ghostly gray.

For the best views across the mountains, many visitors climb to the observation tower at the summit of Clingmans Dome

The region's climate is largely responsible for this visual effect as well as for the name "Smoky Mountains." Positioned in the southeastern U.S., the region receives moist, **temperate** winds from the Gulf of Mexico. This warm, damp air can create a haze that makes it seem as if distant objects are fading away. When that same air combines with the cool air found at higher elevations, the moisture condenses into fog or clouds. In some cases, **transpiration** from very dense clusters of plants in the region condenses into small but thick pockets of fog that hover among the mountain slopes. This creates a distinctive phenomenon in which white or gray "smoke" seems to be issuing from the mountains themselves.

Of course, the Smoky Mountains' climate has a much greater influence on the region than just haze and fog. The higher, cooler elevations of the Great Smoky Mountains receive about 85 inches (216 cm) of rain per year, making them among the wettest areas in the U.S. Frequent downpours result in constantly flowing water throughout the region. As the rivers and streams flow toward valleys and lowlands, they can vary in intensity from powerful waterfalls to swift rapids to lazy pools. The lowest point in the Great Smoky Mountains has an elevation of 875 feet (267 m). This and other low areas are warmer and thus don't cause condensation to the same extent as the higher reaches of the Great Smoky Mountains, but they still receive an ample 50 inches (127 cm) of rain each year on average.

The region's abundance of water is one factor that makes the Great Smoky Mountains one of Earth's most biologically diverse areas outside the tropics, but there are other reasons for this diversity as well. Many millions of years ago, the region that is now Great Smoky Mountains

Roaring Fork (pictured) and the many other streams within the Smoky Mountains can turn suddenly forceful during heavy rains

The little northern saw-whet owl is so named because its whistling call sounds like a saw being sharpened on a whetstone

National Park was warmer, and subtropical plants covered the lowlands, while **temperate forests** covered higher elevations. Then, about a million years ago, an ice age began. As temperatures slowly dropped over thousands of years, plants began growing farther and farther south, near the warmer temperatures they needed to survive. Since most animals relied on these plants for food, the animals also drifted south, which effectively caused entire **ecosystems** to shift. Then, as much of Earth experienced a warming trend about 10,000 years ago, life gradually moved northward again. What is noteworthy about the Great Smoky Mountains region is that it offered some plants and animals an alternative to shifting south or north. Simply by moving down to lower, warmer elevations, many living things were able to withstand colder climates. When the climate heated up again, some life forms in the region retreated to higher, cooler elevations. In this way, various types of plants and animals were able to remain in the region at the same time that climate changes were bringing in new species.

To this day, the highest elevations of the Great Smoky Mountains are home to lichens and mosses that are normally found only in polar locales, and the region's high-altitude forests are home to animals—such as northern flying squirrels, black-capped chickadees, northern saw-whet owls, and common ravens—that are typically found in the northern U.S. or Canada. On the other end of the spectrum, the region's sheltered lowland valleys host an unusually high number of delicate wildflowers and other leafy plants and serve as a summer home to birds from Central and South America.

In all, the Great Smoky Mountains are home to more than 1,600 species of flowering plants. The region also contains many non-flowering species, including various ferns, mosses, and a plant called Rugel's ragwort, which is found nowhere else in the world. About 95 percent of the Great Smoky Mountains region is covered by forest. Five distinctive types of forest—cove hardwood, spruce-fir, northern hardwood, hemlock, and pine-and-oak—can be seen in these mountains, their features the result of differences in elevation, water supply, and soil quality.

The region's variety of plants and abundance of water support varied animal life, including more than 60 different mammals, 200 birds, 50 fish, and 80 reptiles and amphibians, not to mention thousands of insects. Perhaps most prominent among these creatures is the black bear, which was once rare but now thrives in the region and is the iconic species of the Great Smoky Mountains. White-tailed deer are among the more visible mammals in the Smokies, and elk are the area's largest animal. Hundreds of miles of rivers and streams in the area contain fish, including several species of trout and bass. The Great Smoky Mountains are sometimes referred to as the "Salamander Capital of the World," and for good reason. Thirty species of salamander are found in the region, including Jordan's salamander, which lives nowhere else on Earth. Reptile species include various turtles, lizards, and snakes. All told, scientists have documented more than 17,000 species of plant and animal life in the Great Smoky Mountains and believe many have yet to be discovered.

Black-capped chickadees live across much of the U.S., as these small birds can tolerate cold temperatures and have a diverse diet

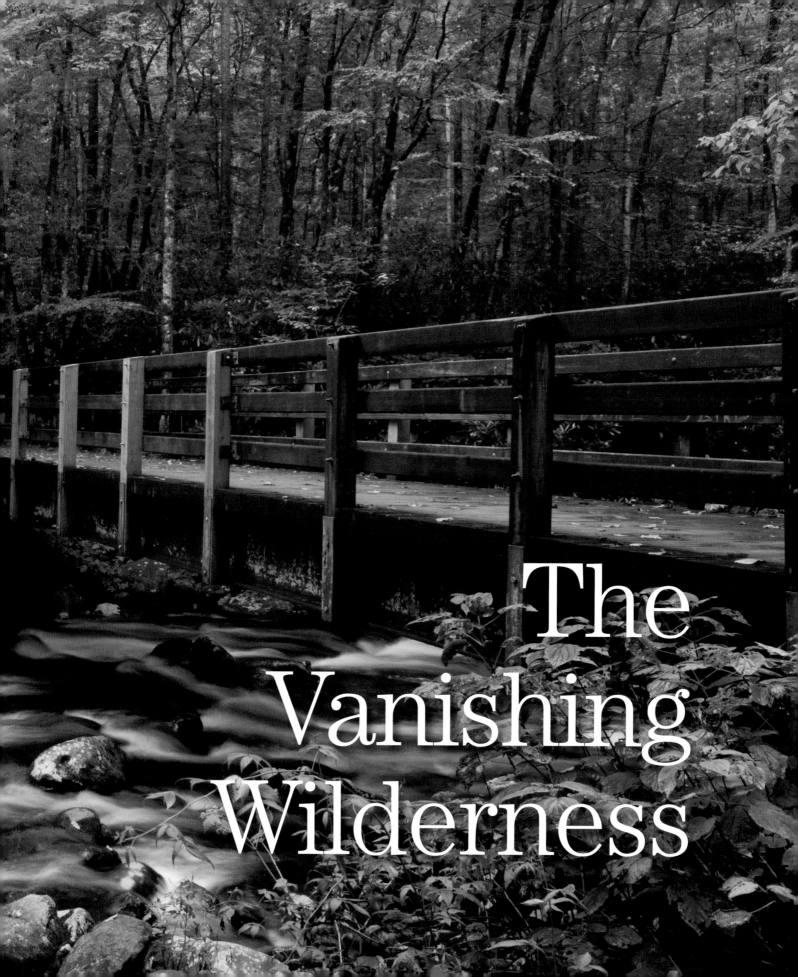

The
Vanishing
Wilderness

Some of the first humans to enter the Great Smoky Mountains region, located at the boundary between present-day Tennessee and North Carolina, may have done so as long as 10,000 years ago. What little evidence remains of early visitors to the area suggests that they were **nomadic** hunters. The relative lack of evidence indicates that permanent settlements were unlikely and the number of people who passed through the area few.

It was closer to 1,000 years ago that people truly began to call the region home. Inhabitants around that time grew plants for food, created pottery, and kept domesticated dogs. Descendants of some of these people came to be known as Cherokee Indians. The first European to see the region may have been Spanish explorer Hernando de Soto, who encountered mountain-dwelling Cherokees in 1540. At that time, the American Indians had small villages along streams with permanent log dwellings, farmlands, and trail systems. The Cherokees had adapted well to the region, but life in the mountains was not easy, and it wasn't until many years later, at the end of the 1700s, that white settlers took up residence in the Smoky Mountains.

While there was some friction between the settlers and Cherokees, the two groups shared the region in relative peace for a few decades. Many of the new settlers lacked knowledge of the wilderness, and it was only by emulating the self-sufficient Indians that they were able to survive. In the 1790s, the first whites reached Cades Cove and Oconaluftee— valleys that would become home to some of the first settlement communities in the mountains. As more settlers came to the region, the Cherokees were pressured to

Settlers pushed Cherokee Indians from the Smokies; later, settlers and Indians clashed again over Oklahoma land called the Cherokee Strip

give up more and more land. By the end of 1838, settlers had claimed virtually all available land in the area and—backed by the U.S. military—forced most of the Cherokees of the region onto a reservation in what is now Oklahoma. Many Cherokees died during the grueling, 1,000-mile (1,610 km) march that became known as the "Trail of Tears."

Over time, life for settlers in the Smoky Mountains shifted from a rugged, wilderness existence to one more reminiscent of farming villages. In addition to hunting for food, locals raised livestock. They cleared larger areas of forest in order to grow corn and other crops, and they built mills and plows. Instead of families fending for themselves and living in isolated cabins, people lived in communities with churches and schools.

In the early 1900s, the growing lumber industry in and around the Great Smoky Mountains again changed people's way of life. Many residents sold their land to the lumber companies and left the region, and many of those who remained worked for the companies. Instead

This barn, reconstructed to 19th-century form, sits in a cove in the Great Smoky Mountains that was once occupied by Cherokees

of producing most of their own goods and meeting their own needs within the villages, locals began working for money, which they used to buy food and manufactured products from stores. Logging towns such as Elkmont, Smokemont, Tremont, and Proctor were built within the Smoky Mountains, and railroad tracks stretched across the region to transport lumber from walnut, spruce, chestnut, pine, hemlock, and any other trees of value. Loggers began clearing the longstanding forests.

By the early 1920s, most of what is now Great Smoky Mountains National Park was cleared of trees. It was around this time that the idea of preserving the Smoky Mountains as a national park began to gain momentum. A resident of the mountains, Horace Kephart, had authored a book about life in the region years earlier, and he was among the first to express concern about the rapidly changing landscape. Yet, well-spoken as he was, it took time for his voice to be heard, and it wasn't until politicians and wealthy businessmen such as Ben Morton and David Chapman had thrown their support behind the idea that it was truly taken seriously. As the popularity of new national parks such as Acadia and Grand Canyon increased, people living in Tennessee and North Carolina began to realize the aesthetic and economic value of the Great Smoky Mountains—a region in their own backyard that they had long taken for granted.

Before the mid-1920s, most national parks had been established in the western U.S. on public land. The NPS wanted to create a national park in the eastern U.S., but that brought extra challenges. The eastern side of America was much more populated than the western, which meant that finding relatively untouched, unowned, and unsettled land was difficult. The Great Smoky Mountains were none of those things, and obtaining land that was already owned and settled was expensive. Approximately 7,000 people lived in the Smoky Mountains, and with the lumber industry booming, the land's value was high.

In 1926, the U.S. Congress approved the establishment of a national park in the Smoky Mountains, but this authorization alone did not ensure success. The NPS did not have the funds needed to buy the land. Instead, the money would have to come from the states of Tennessee and North Carolina and from private donors. In 1928, **philanthropist** John D. Rockefeller Jr.—whose family had made its fortune in the oil industry—offered to donate $5 million toward the development of the park, provided the states could raise the same amount for the cause. It took a few years, but the necessary funds were raised, and Rockefeller's donation was collected.

Even with the monetary means to purchase the land, convincing all landowners to give up their claims was not easy. Lumber companies

Fall is a season of great beauty in the Smokies, as changing leaf colors complement the blue haze and gray fog of the mountains

While logging remains an active industry within the Appalachian Mountains, it has long been banned within the Smoky Mountains

did not mind selling as long as the price was right, but for many homesteaders who had lived in the Smoky Mountains for generations, money was a poor tradeoff for their way of life. Nonetheless, the U.S. government was backing the new national park, and 1,200 residents within its borders were ordered to leave their homes and accept buyouts.

On June 15, 1934, Great Smoky Mountains National Park was officially established. The park was irregularly shaped, its boundaries following the contours of rivers and mountains. It was roughly 40 miles (64 km) from east to west and 20 miles (32 km) north to south, and its 814 square miles (2,108 sq km) were evenly split between Tennessee and North Carolina. Approximately two-thirds of the park had already been deforested. Fortunately, lumber companies had generally targeted the larger, mature trees, and the areas of forest left standing still contained most of the region's plant diversity. Although deforestation had become a serious threat to the local ecosystem, new forests would grow again, with most of the plant and animal species still present.

The park's beginnings coincided with the peak of the Great Depression, and with jobs scarce nationwide, government programs such as the Civilian Conservation Corps (CCC) were created. The CCC combined work relief with conservation and created jobs specifically for young, unmarried men who would construct and maintain buildings, roads, fire towers, and bridges. The organization also worked to improve natural lands by planting trees, managing erosion, guarding against forest fires, and monitoring water quality. The CCC was largely responsible for many of the Great Smoky Mountains' first official park buildings and trails.

Old roadways and railways in the park were easily converted to park roads, many of the logging towns were converted into campgrounds, and most of the civilian buildings were torn down. However, in some of the oldest villages, such as Cades Cove, Oconaluftee, Cataloochee, and Roaring Fork, some structures dating as far back as the early 1800s were left standing and given maintenance, even as the forests slowly grew back around them. In this way, Great Smoky Mountains National Park became not only a natural preserve but a cultural one as well.

The John Cable Grist Mill, constructed along creeks in 1868, is one of a dozen preserved historical structures in Cades Cove

Turning Back the Clock

The Smokies have suffered the arrival of pests such as garlic mustard (below) and the elimination of animals such as river otters (right)

When Great Smoky Mountains National Park was established, it was unique among America's 26 total national parks. Other parks had originated in a predominantly natural setting, and management of those parks involved maintaining that undisturbed environment while making the area accessible to tourists. By contrast, human activity in the Great Smoky Mountains had greatly compromised the naturalness of the region before the park existed. As a result, the initial challenge of managing Great Smoky Mountains National Park was to return the land back to its original state.

Even though logging and hunting were banned in the national park, the prior destruction of habitat, along with hunting and trapping in the region, had already wiped out animals such as bison, elk, mountain lions, wolves, river otters, and peregrine falcons. Until trees grew back, there would be little chance of those animals ever making a comeback. And while park officials waited for the forests to recover, nonnative species emerged as a threat to native plants and animals.

Since European settlers first arrived, more than 380 nonnative plants have been introduced to the Great Smoky Mountains. About 35 of those—including the garlic mustard plant—spread very rapidly and can choke out native plants that are important to the ecosystem. Some nonnative species were introduced when Europeans brought seeds or plants with them from their homelands. Other seeds have entered the region in dirt used for construction projects or have been inadvertently carried in by tourists. Today, park workers spend thousands of hours each year monitoring and clearing out the invading plants.

Rainbow trout and brown trout were commonly stocked as game fish in the Great Smoky Mountains' streams beginning in the early 1900s. Park management itself stocked the fish from 1934 to 1975. The region's only native trout are brook trout, and their numbers and range shrank dramatically as the nonnative fish took over the waterways. Although efforts have been made in recent years to remove nonnative trout, progress is slow, and only small stretches of river in the park have been restored as native habitats.

The wild hog is another nonnative inhabitant of the park. Wild hogs are native to Europe and likely entered the Smoky Mountains in the 1920s when some of the animals escaped from a game farm. Over the decades, wild hogs have spread, and domestic pigs, which descended from wild hogs, have often escaped from farms and become feral—reverting to an appearance and behavior similar to that of their wild ancestors. Whether truly wild or feral, both types are hardy, will eat just about anything, give birth to large litters, and have almost no predators to keep their population down. The hogs tear up important plant-growing areas as they root for food and wallow in soft soil, and they prey upon small animals, including rare salamander species. Although park workers in the Great Smoky Mountains trap or shoot hundreds of the destructive animals each year, hog numbers remain high.

Although the park has "hog teams" trained in the removal of wild hogs, total elimination of these invaders is unlikely

While the swift peregrine falcon (above) is again at home in the Smokies, the shy red wolf (below) failed to make a comeback

Much smaller creatures are an even bigger concern to park officials today. Woolly adelgids are tiny insects almost too small to see. Yet, over time, these diminutive transplants from Europe and Asia can kill some of the largest evergreen trees in the world by damaging their needles and disrupting the process by which the trees convert the sun's energy into food. Balsam woolly adelgids reached the Great Smoky Mountains in 1962 and have since killed more than 90 percent of the park's mature Fraser firs. Hemlock woolly adelgids appeared in the region in 2002 and have spread throughout the park, threatening its tallest and oldest trees. Hemlocks in the Smoky Mountains can grow more than 150 feet (46 m) tall, and some have lived more than 500 years. Efforts to stop the insects have included treating trees with insecticides and releasing adelgid-eating beetles into the park. And while there have been some signs of success, the battle against these bugs continues.

By the early 1990s—about six decades after Great Smoky Mountains National Park was established—many of the park's forests had grown back enough to allow for the reintroduction of animals previously exterminated from the area. River otters and peregrine falcons were successfully reintroduced to the park and have again found their niche in the ecosystem. Similar attempts to reintroduce the critically endangered red wolf, on the other hand, were not successful, as the wolves failed to maintain a sustainable population.

In 2001, an experimental elk reintroduction program began at the park, starting with 25 transplanted animals the first year and an additional 27 in 2002. Park officials closely studied the small elk herds, which inhabited southeastern pockets of the park, to monitor how they

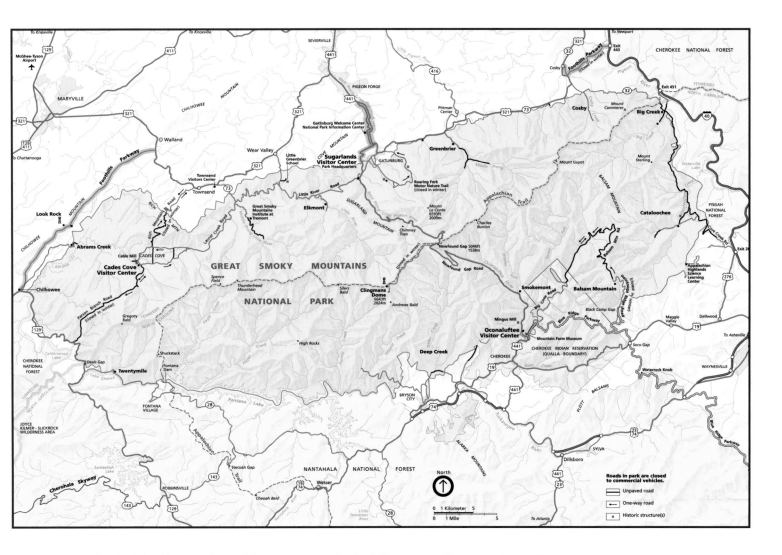

adapted to the park and how they affected the overall ecosystem. By the time the study concluded in 2008, more than 100 elk were thriving in Great Smoky Mountains National Park. As of 2012, the park's elk remained closely monitored, and while the large ear tags they wore were a reminder that the program was still a work in progress, the animals' reintroduction was tentatively considered a success.

Air quality is another ongoing concern in Great Smoky Mountains National Park, which is considered the most polluted park in the U.S. The same Gulf of Mexico winds that carry in warm moisture also carry in pollution from miles away—pollution that becomes trapped in the area's thick, damp air. The burning of coal, oil, or gas in factories and automobiles releases harmful sulfate particles and gases that get

This map illustrates the scarcity of roads and abundance of creeks throughout Great Smoky Mountains National Park

Spending the night in the Smokies often means tenting, as the park lacks permanent lodging and is not overly RV-friendly

caught in the natural mist of the region. Since 1948, these particles have reduced visibility in the Smokies by more than half, affecting not only how far one can see but also reducing visible color. The air pollution also creates **acid rain** and **ozone**, both of which harm vegetation in the park, especially at higher altitudes. High amounts of ozone can also cause respiratory problems in people.

Because virtually all of the park's air pollution originates outside park borders, that is where solutions to the problem have been sought. Since 1980, the NPS has had a voice regarding where factories and power plants may be built and what levels of emissions are acceptable in areas that affect the Great Smoky Mountains. Even so, the concentration of sulfate particles has continued to rise, and park management continues to face an uphill battle against the problem.

One non-change to the park that frequently generates discussion is the lack of tourism-friendly upgrades. As sizeable as the park is, Great Smoky Mountains' roads are limited in number, and driving from one point in the park to another often requires visitors to make extensive use

of roadways outside park boundaries. The limited road space, combined with huge numbers of visitors, can mean slow-moving, bumper-to-bumper traffic or circling packed parking lots around popular areas such as Cades Cove and Clingmans Dome. In-park shuttle bus services have been proposed, but no such option currently exists.

The park's services are also very basic compared with those of some of America's other popular national parks. Yellowstone National Park has more than 2,000 hotel rooms and cabins where visitors may stay. As of 2012, Great Smoky Mountains had 10. There are no showers in the park, no electricity in campgrounds (or in the cabins), and no RV hookups. While some visitors would prefer a more "developed" park, an emphasis on minimizing human impact has kept the park relatively primitive, and gateway towns such as Gatlinburg (Tennessee), Townsend (Tennessee), and Bryson City (North Carolina) greatly benefit from the tourist traffic outside the park and from those visitors who want more comfortable lodging.

The Great Smoky Mountains are notable for their winding roads, long views, and proximity to historic towns such as Gatlinburg

A Metropolitan Oasis

Great Smoky Mountains National Park is far and away the most visited national park in the U.S. Each year, it receives around 9 million visitors, more than twice as many as any other park. The primary reasons for its popularity are its location and climate. The Smoky Mountains are nestled among one of the more densely populated portions of America and can easily be reached by car in one day from such big cities as Charlotte, Memphis, Nashville, Louisville, and Atlanta. It is also among the closer national park options for residents of Washington, D.C., Philadelphia, and New York. Some tourists travel across the country to visit the Great Smoky Mountains for an extended period of time, but most visitors to the park live relatively close and may visit for a weekend or even a single day.

The Smoky Mountains' southerly location and temperate Gulf winds make for weather that is pleasant much of the year. At lower elevations, the average high temperatures range from 88 °F (31 °C) in midsummer to 51 °F (11 °C) in midwinter. Even in January and February, snow accumulation is uncommon in the park's valleys and lowlands.

Great Smoky Mountains National Park can be enjoyed by people with many different interests. For tourists who stick to the roadways, the park's winding roads pass by various scenic overlooks, including

This view from Clingmans Dome depicts a horizon made blue by haze, as well as dying trees affected by woolly adelgids

the popular Newfound Gap, which, at an elevation of 5,048 feet (1,539 m), allows visitors to gaze across miles of green mountain slopes and pockets of mist. Those who want an even higher vantage point can travel an extra seven miles (11 km) upward toward Clingmans Dome.

Other popular driving tours include the picturesque Cades Cove in the western reaches of the park and Cataloochee near the eastern edge. Early settlements existed in each area, and both contain historic buildings such as churches, cabins, mills, and schools. These low valleys are also among the few places in the park that are not completely forested, so they offer some of the best opportunities to spot wildlife in what is otherwise a very animal-concealing park. A visitor's chances of seeing black bears are better near Cades Cove, while elk are isolated near Cataloochee. Deer, wild turkeys, and smaller animals are frequently seen in either location. Mornings and evenings are typically the best times to spot wildlife.

Clockwise, sightseeing images from Cades Cove: a historic church, a water-powered grist mill, wild turkeys feeding

The Smokies have an abundance of hiking trails, including the legendary Appalachian Trail, which runs the length of the park

The park's roadways also pass close to picnic areas, various streams, and lush stretches of wildflowers. Naturally, they lead directly to the park's three visitor centers—Cades Cove, Sugarlands, and Oconaluftee—where tourists can learn about the park, register for camping, or shop for books, trail maps, and souvenirs.

Visitors who are willing to stretch their legs a little have many more options than those who restrict themselves to vehicles. The most common activity in the park is hiking, and Great Smoky Mountains contains more than 800 miles (1,287 km) of trails, including a 70-mile (113 km) segment of the famous Appalachian Trail, which runs all the way from Georgia to Maine. Trails often begin at or pass by many of the same attractions that can be reached by car, but trails lead to many locations vehicles cannot get near. Whether hikers want to follow the spine of a mountain, visit the remains of an old mountain dwelling, or wander among 500-year-old hemlock trees, there are routes that allow them to do so.

The park's trails are not just for hardcore hikers. Some of Great Smoky Mountains' trails are less than a mile (1.6 km) long, and visitors can find many short, often paved, paths just off the roadways that lead to scenic overlooks or impressive waterfalls such as Laurel Falls and Grotto Falls. The most common "hike" in the park is possibly the short but steep half-mile (800 m) trek from the parking lot near Clingmans

*Laurel Falls, which
falls 80 feet (24 m)
and is split into an
upper and lower
section, is one of
the biggest tourist
draws in the park*

With more than 700 miles (1,130 km) of fishable streams in the park, Smoky Mountains anglers can pursue trout in relative solitude

Dome to the lookout structure built atop the peak. From this, the highest point in the park—more than 6,600 feet (2,012 m) above sea level—visitors can get a 360-degree view of the region. Some days, people can see as far as 100 miles (160 km). Other days, observers are completely enveloped in clouds.

Other methods of traversing the Great Smoky Mountains include horseback riding and bicycling. Horse riding services are offered by **concessionaires** in four locations around the park. The pacing of the rides is suitable for beginners, and trips range from 45 minutes to multiple hours. Some locations also offer carriage rides or hayrides. Visitors can also bring their own horses to the park's five horse camps, which provide access to horse-approved hiking trails. About 550 miles (885 km) of trails are open for riding, and visitors can obtain horse-trail maps within the park.

Bicycles are allowed on most roads within the park, but steep slopes, blind curves, and heavy traffic present safety concerns in many areas. The most noteworthy exception is the 11-mile (18 km) Loop Road at Cades Cove. The relatively flat terrain, high visibility, and one-way traffic make this road a safe and pleasant route, and the nearby Cades Cove campground store rents out bikes during the summer and fall. Great Smoky Mountains National Park does not have mountain bike trails, and bicycles are not allowed on hiking trails.

The Smoky Mountains' rivers and streams are another source of recreation. Anglers can pursue trout and bass year round, provided they have a Tennessee or North Carolina fishing license, either of which allows fishing anywhere in the park. In the interests of keeping rivers free from unwanted organisms and minimizing harm to caught-and-released fish, only artificial flies and fishing lures with single hooks may be used. Rainbow and brook trout in the Smoky Mountains rarely grow longer than eight inches (20 cm), but brown trout can be significantly larger.

Family-friendly and requiring no skill or experience, tubing is a popular summer recreation in and near the park

Other recreational uses of the park's rivers include tubing and kayaking, and concessionaires in nearby towns rent out hundreds of inflatable tubes. Customers are shuttled to higher elevations and ride the river back down, or they may float downstream first and be shuttled back up to the starting point. Typical rides last 60 to 90 minutes. Sections of streams that are too calm for tubing can be ideal for swimming beaches, and in midsummer, some of the park's broader, slower streams bustle with swimmers, sunbathers, and picnickers.

For guests needing a place to sleep during their stay, Great Smoky Mountains National Park has 10 drive-in campgrounds for RV and tent campers, with nearly 1,000 campsites in all, including large group sites. The campgrounds have cold running water and flush toilets but few other amenities. The park also has more than 100 **backcountry** sites. While some of the park's campsites can be had on a first-come, first-served basis, many require reservations. Some of the larger campgrounds have small stores where visitors can buy firewood as well as basic food, camping, and general use items.

The only indoor lodging structures in the park are at LeConte Lodge, which features 10 rustic cabins and a dining hall. The lodge, located in the north-central portion of the park, dates back to 1926—before the national park existed—and is both hard to reach and to book. Hikers must trek five miles (8 km) to reach the mountain settlement, and cabins often must be reserved up to a year in advance. The shortage of cabins or inns and the lack of electricity and showers in the campgrounds surprise many visitors, but overnight accommodations are readily available in nearby towns such as Gatlinburg, Tennessee, and Cherokee, North Carolina.

Many people view the fact that Great Smoky Mountains National Park does not have the modern amenities of other national parks as a sign of success. After all, this is a park that, less than a century ago, was a landscape nearing complete deforestation. Today, having returned close to their natural form, the misty and mysterious Great Smoky Mountains draw millions of visitors who can gain a greater appreciation for the forested hills and abundant streams, as well as the way people once lived modestly among them.

Because kayaks are light in weight and shallow in design, they are good watercraft for navigating small rivers and streams

Mascot of the Smokies

The Great Smoky Mountains are among the few places in the eastern U.S. where black bears still live in the wild, and approximately 1,500 of them are found in the park today. In the summer, mature males may weigh 250 pounds (113 kg), while females are typically less than half that size. By late fall, though, bears may double that weight ahead of the colder winter months, when the berries, nuts, and plants that make up a bear's diet are in short supply. Despite their bulk, black bears are nimble creatures that can climb trees, swim well, and run up to 30 miles (48 km) per hour.

Getting a Second Chance

The largest animals in the park, elk have become a favorite of tourists since the species was reintroduced into the Great Smoky Mountains in 2001. Like other members of the deer family, elk are adaptable to various environments and are found in many countries throughout the world. Male elk, called bulls, in the park weigh up to 700 pounds (318 kg) and grow antlers more than 3 feet (91 cm) long. These antlers are shed and regrown annually. Most elk live in herds and prefer forest habitats, but they often feed at the edge of forests where shrubs and grasses offer more food options than forest interiors.

Mountaintop Hike

Mount LeConte, which reaches 6,593 feet (2,010 m), is the park's tallest mountain in terms of distance from base to peak, and found along its slopes is the Alum Cave Trail. This path is often steep and winds along various streams, old forests, and cliffs. The first quarter of the five-mile (8 km) trail leads to Arch Rock, an ancient stone tunnel formed by years of erosion. Another mile (1.6 km) farther are the Alum Cave Bluffs, which feature high, sheer walls and inspiring vantage points of the surrounding landscape. Hikers who follow the entire trail toward the mountaintop are rewarded with unique scenery and perhaps a stay at the rustic Mount LeConte Lodge.

Cades Cove Hayride

The Cades Cove Loop Road is among the most popular tourist destinations in the Smoky Mountains. It's so popular, in fact, that the traffic flow may feel like rush hour in a big city. A low-stress alternative is to take a ranger-led hayride around the loop. The horse-drawn wagons provide uninhibited views of the open valley and surrounding mountains and pass near the historic buildings of the area. Throughout the tour, a ranger will share information about the park's natural and cultural history as well as details about the Smoky Mountains today. All the while, passengers can gaze at scenery and wildlife instead of brake lights.

Whitewater Recreation

About 60 miles (97 km) northwest of Great Smoky Mountains National Park and just west of the Appalachian Mountains lies Big South Fork National River and Recreation Area. Big South Fork encompasses nearly 200 square miles (518 sq km) and features a 40-mile-long (64 km) gorge cut by the Cumberland River. The area is popular for its whitewater rapids, which offer thrilling opportunities for rafters, kayakers, and other water sport enthusiasts. In addition to hiking, horseback riding, fishing, and camping, Big South Fork also permits mountain biking and hunting for deer, wild boar, turkey, and small game—activities not allowed in Great Smoky Mountains National Park.

Remembering a President

The Andrew Johnson National Historic Site is located about 40 miles (64 km) northeast of Great Smoky Mountains National Park, near

Greeneville, Tennessee. Originally established as a national monument in 1935, the site honors the 17th U.S. president, who was in office from 1865 to 1869 and faced with many difficult tasks following the assassination of Abraham Lincoln and the end of the Civil War. The historic site features Andrew Johnson's tailor shop, where he worked as a young man; a home, with original furnishings, where he lived for 24 years; a museum detailing Johnson's life before, during, and after his presidency; and the cemetery where he is buried.

Staying on Course

Hiking in the Great Smoky Mountains' backcountry can lead to many breathtaking vistas and unexpected wonders, but the dense forests and miles of uniform mountain peaks can turn frightening to the hiker who becomes lost. Hiking alone is not advised, and someone not participating in the hike should know where hikers are going (cell phone reception is unreliable amid mountains). Having trail maps and knowing how to read them is also a must, and hikers should be at a backcountry campsite or off the trails before dark. Carrying extra water, flashlights, and warm, rain-resistant clothing are wise precautions to take in the event a hike turns into a survival situation.

Unwanted Dinner Guests

While black bears are naturally wary of humans, they may overcome their inhibitions if food is easily accessible. Campers in the Great Smoky Mountains are required to store food in vehicles or "bear-proof" containers overnight, and food waste must be placed in special dumpsters. Park rangers even advise against spitting toothpaste on the ground. Of course, visitors should never deliberately give food to bears they see throughout

the park. Bears that find human food or receive handouts can quickly become dependent upon them. Bears that lose their fear of humans are potentially dangerous, and unfortunately, park management is forced to kill several such bears every year.

Glossary

acid rain: rain that is acidic, formed when emissions from burned fossil fuels combine with moisture in the atmosphere

backcountry: an area that is away from developed or populated areas

concessionaires: people or organizations who operate businesses on sites owned by someone else

conifers: trees or shrubs usually having needle-shaped or scalelike leaves and seed-producing cones

continental drift: the theory that continents slowly change location on Earth's surface as they drift on molten rock within the planet

ecosystems: communities of animals, plants, and other living things interacting together within an environment

eroded: worn away by the action of natural forces such as water, wind, or ice

faults: prominent breaks in the rock layers that make up Earth's crust; shifts or fractures may happen there, causing earthquakes or the growth of mountains

nomadic: describing people who move frequently to new locations in order to obtain food, water, and shelter

ozone: an unstable form of oxygen that can cause harmful reactions within organisms when inhaled or absorbed

philanthropist: a person, usually of wealth, who makes an active effort to improve society or human welfare

tectonic plates: the enormous slabs of earth that shift during continental drift

temperate: describing a moderate climate that lacks extreme shifts in temperature

temperate forests: forests that contain leafy plants, or a combination of leafy and coniferous plants, and that can endure a moderate range of hot and cold temperatures

transpiration: the process by which plants release water vapor

Selected Bibliography

Brewer, Carson, and Ken Jenkins. *Great Smoky Mountains National Park*. Portland, Ore.: Graphic Arts Center, 1993.

Carlton, Mike, and John Netherton. *Great Smoky Mountains National Park: Wildlife Watcher's Guide*. Minocqua, Wis.: NorthWord Press, 1996.

Great Smoky Mountains National Park. New York: Fodor's Travel, 2009.

National Geographic Guide to the National Parks of the United States. Washington, D.C.: National Geographic Society, 2009.

Schullery, Paul. *America's National Parks: The Spectacular Forces That Shaped Our Treasured Lands*. New York: DK Publishing, 2001.

Toops, Connie. *Great Smoky Mountains*. Stillwater, Minn.: Voyageur Press, 1992.

White, Mel. *Complete National Parks of the United States*. Washington, D.C.: National Geographic Society, 2009.

Websites

Great Smoky Mountains National Park
http://www.nps.gov/grsm/index.htm
The official National Park Service site for the Great Smoky Mountains is the most complete online source for information on the park and includes tips on viewing wildlife.

National Geographic: Great Smoky Mountains National Park
http://travel.nationalgeographic.com/travel/national-parks/great-smoky-mountains-national-park/
This site provides a concise visitor's guide to the Great Smoky Mountains, complete with maps, photos, sightseeing suggestions, and links to other popular national parks.

Index